A

CATALOGUE

OF

INDIAN MEDICINAL

PLANTS AND DRUGS

A

CATALOGUE

OF

INDIAN MEDICINAL

PLANTS AND DRUGS,

WITH THEIR NAMES IN THE

Hindustani and Sanscrit Languages.

BY

JOHN FLEMING

GYAN

Published by

GYAN

Gyan Publishing House
5, Ansari Road
Daryaganj, New Delhi-110002
Phone: 011-47034999, 9811692060
E-mail: books@gyanbooks.com

Distribution Network
gyanbooks.com
India, USA, Canada, UK, Australia

ISBN: 978-93-6280-772-4 (PB)
First Published, 1810

2nd Impression 2024

Printed at: Gyan Press, Delhi.

A CATALOGUE OF INDIAN MEDICINAL PLANTS AND DRUGS
Author: JOHN FLEMING

A

CATALOGUE

OF

INDIAN MEDICINAL

PLANTS AND DRUGS,

WITH THEIR NAMES IN THE

Hindustani and Sunscrit Languages.

BY JOHN FLEMING, M. D.

SURGEON ON THE BENGAL ESTABLISHMENT.

Calcutta:

PRINTED AT THE HINDUSTANI PRESS,

BY A. H. HUBBARD.

1812.

ERRATA.

Page.	Line.	*for*	*read*
18....	15....	power,	powder.
20....	15....	CRISTIE,	CHRISTIE.
26....	9....	small,	tall.
33....	16....	*Hindu,*	*Indian.*
59....	2....	*Autennæ,*	*Antennæ.*
64....	4....	33d.	53d.

Advertisement.

THE following catalogue is intended chiefly for the use of gentlemen of the medical profession on their first arrival in *India*, to whom it must be desirable to know what articles of the *Materia Medica* this country affords, and by what names they may find them.

The *systematic* names of the plants are taken from WILLDENOW's edition of the *Species Plantarum* L. with the exception of some new species, not included in that work, which have been arranged in the system, and described by Dr. ROXBURGH; who, with his usual liberality, permitted me to transcribe their specific characters and trivial names from his manuscript.

In ascertaining and fixing the *Hindustáni* and *Sanscrit* names which correspond to the *systematic*, a point of considerable difficulty, but essential for the purpose of this catalogue, I have been greatly assisted by Mr. COLEBROOKE, on whose thorough acquaintance with oriental literature, as well as his knowledge in botany, I knew that I could confidently rely.

The *Hindustáni* and *Sanscrit* words are expressed in *Roman* characters, conformably to the system of notation recommended by Sir WILLIAM JONES; but as many prefer, for the *Hindustáni*, the system of Mr. GILCHRIST, the names in that language are printed according to his orthography, at the bottom of the page.

For the virtues and uses of such medicinal plants and drugs as are already well known in *Europe*, I have judged it sufficient to refer to the two latest and best works on the Materia Medica, MURRAY'S "Apparatus Medicaminum,"* and WOODVILLE'S "Medical Botany."† Of the qualities of those articles which are known only in this country, some account is now offered; which, however brief and imperfect, will, it is hoped, have at least the effect of promoting further inquiry.

---

* Apparatus Medicaminum &c. Auctore JO. ANDREA MURRAY. Tom. VI. 8. *Gotting.* 1790.

† Medical Botany &c. By WILLIAM WOODVILLE, M. D. 4 vols. 4to. *Lond.* 1794.

I. *MEDICINAL PLANTS.*

ABRUS. PRECATORIUS. (W.) *Guncha*(1) H. *Gunjá* S.
The Seed. *Retti*(2) H. *Racticá* S.

THE root of this plant, when dried, coincides very exactly, in appearance and medicinal qualities, with the liquorice root, and is often sold for it in the bazars.

See *Glycyrrhiza Glabra* { MURRAY II. 457
WOODVILLE III. 458

The lowest weight in use among the *Hindû* druggists takes its denomination of *Retti* from the seed of the *Gunjá*, though the fictitious weight is nearly double that of the seed. Sir WILLIAM JONES found, from the average of numerous trials, the weight of one *Gunjá* seed to be a grain and five sixteenths. The *Retti* weight used by the jewellers and druggists is equal to two grains three sixteenths nearly. See Asiatick Researches II. p. 154. and V. p. 92.

(1) *Gooncha.* (2) *Ruttee.*

Acacia Arabica. (W.) *Babúl*(1) H. *Barbúra* S.
The Gum. *Babúl-ca Gúnd*(2) H.

The *Acacia vera* (W.) (*Mimosa Nilotica* L.) which yields the *Gummi Arabicum* of the *European* pharmacopœias, is not found among the numerous species of *Acacias* that are natives of *Hindustan;* but the gum of the *Babúl* is so perfectly similar to gum Arabic, that, for every purpose, whether medicinal or economical, it may be substituted for it. The bark of the tree, like that of most of the *Acacias*, is a powerful astringent; and is used, instead of oak bark, for tanning, by the *European* manufacturers of leather in *Bengal.*

For *Mimosa Nilotica* See { Murray, II. 528. / Woodville, II. 187.

Acacia Catechu. (W.) *K'hayar*(3) H. *C'hadira* S.
Mimosa Cate Murray, II. 540.
Mimosa Catechu Woodville, II. 183.

Acorus Calamus. (W.) *Bach*(4) H. *Vachá* S.
Murray, V. 39.
Woodville, III. 472.

Allium Sativum. (W.) *Lehsen*(5) H. *Lasúna* S.
Murray, V. 122.
Woodville, III. 472.

Aloe Perfoliata. (W.) *Ghí-Cumár*(6) H. *Ghrita-Cumári* [and *Taruni* S.
The Gum. *Elwa*(7) H. *Mus'ebber*(8) Arab.
Murray, V. 238.
Woodville, III. 556.

---

(1) *Bubool.* (2) *Bubool-ka Goond.* (3) *K,huer.* (4) *Buch.*
(5) *Luhsun.* (6) *G,heekoowar.* (7) *Elwa.* (8) *Moosubbur.*

Amomum Cardamomum. (W.) *Iláchi*(1) H. *Elá* S.

Amomum Cardamomum. Murray, V. 61.

Amomum Repens. Woodville, II. 356.

Amomum Zingiber. (W.) *Adrac*(2) H. *Ardraca* S.

The dried root, *Sont'h* H. *Sunt'hi* S.

Murray, V. 52.

Woodville, I. 31.

Andropogon Schoenanthus. (W.) *Gendbél*(3) H. *B'hús-* [*trĭna* S.

Murray, V. 443.

This plant, under the name of *Juncus odoratus,* had formerly a place in all the *European* pharmacopœias, but it is now rarely met with in the shops. It continues, however, to be a favourite herb with the *Asiaticks,* both for medicinal and culinary purposes. The *Hindù* practitioners consider the infusion of the leaves as sudorific, diuretic and emmenagogue. Whatever title it may have to these virtues, it is at least a very agreeable diluent ; and, on account of it's fragant smell, aromatic flavour, and warm, bitterish, but not unpleasant taste, is generally found to be a drink very grateful to the stomach in sickness. Many *Europeans,* with whom tea does not agree, use, instead of it, the infusion of this plant, to which they have given the name of lemon-grass.

Anethum Sowa (Roxb. MS.) *Sówá*(4) H. *Mísréyá* S.

Sp. Ch.—Annual. Leaves superdecompound. Umbel of 5—15 equally elevated radii. Fruit oblong, flat. Seeds without a membranaceous margin, and with three ribs on the base.

---

(1) *Ilachee.* (2) *Udruk.* (3) *Gundbel.* (4) *Soä.*

Anethum Panmorium (Roxb. MS.) *Mayuri*(1) H. *Mad'hurica* S.

Sp. Ch.—Annual. Erect. Ramous. Leaves superdecompound. Umbel of from 10 to 20 unequally elevated radii. Fruit oblong, deeply furrowed, but not winged.

The former of these umbelliferous plants resembles in appearance the *Anethum graveolens* (W.) and the other the *Anethum fœniculum* (W.) Both species are cultivated in *Bengal*, on account of their seeds, which are used in diet, as well as in medicine. They are warm aromatics, and may supply the places of dill and fennel-seed, as carminatives, in cases of flatulent colic or dyspepsia.

Apium Involucratum (Roxb. MS.) *Ajmud*(2) H. *Ajamòda* S.

Sp. Ch.—Annual. Glaucous. Villous. Superior leaflets filiform. Both general and partial involucra about six leaved.

This species of *Apium* is cultivated in *Bengal* for the seeds only, the natives never using the leaves. The seeds have a very agreeable aromatic flavour, and are therefore much employed in diet as a condiment. They are also used in medicine, in the same cases as the *Sowa* and *Mayuri* seeds above mentioned.

Argemone Mexicana (W.) *Bherbánd*,(3) and *Shial Cántá*.(4) H.

The seed of this plant is used in the *West Indies* as a substitute for ipecacuan. Dr. Grainger assures us that, " where ipecacuan is not at hand,

(1) *Muyooree.* (2) *Ujmood.* (3) *Bhurbanr.* (4) *Shial-kanta.*

"the following emetic may be depended on. "Bruise two drachms of yellow thistle seed, (*Argemone Mexicana*) and infuse it in half a gill of "boiling water. Let it stand till it cools, then "strain and sweeten it to the palate. This is a "sufficient dose for a grown up negroe. The yel-"low thistle seed is not only a safe emetic, but, "like the ipecacuan, is a strengthener of the sto-"mach."

Essay on W. Ind. Dis. page 35.—*2d Edit. Edinb.* 1802.

The *Argemone Mexicana* is one of the commonest weeds in *Hindustan,* and one of the most troublesome to the husbandman: yet there is reason to believe that it is not a native of this country, but brought hither, accidentally from *America* by the *Portuguese,* as it was by the *Spaniards* to *Europe,* in the southern countries of which it now grows wild. This seems the more probable from its not having any name in the *Sanscrit* language, or in the *Persian,* and from its not being noticed, though a very specious plant, either by VAN RHEEDE or by RUMPHIUS.

The seed is not used in medicine by the native practitioners, nor as far as I know has it ever been tried here by the *European.* There can be no reason, however, for not having recourse to it in the case of a deficience of *ipecacuan,* especially as we may rest assured, on so unexceptionable an authority as that above cited, that the experiment would not be attended with any risk.

Aristolochia Indica. (W.) *Isármel,*(1) H.

The root of this species of birthwort is intensely bitter, and is supposed by the *Hindus* to possess the emmenagogue and antarthritic virtues which were formerly ascribed in *Europe* to its congeners, the Aristolochia longa and rotunda. As its bitterness is accompanied with a considerable degree of aromatic warmth, it will probably be found a useful medicine in dyspepsia.

Artemisia Vulgaris. (W.) *Nág-dóna* H. *Nágadamana* S.
Murray, I. 190.
Woodville, II. 331.

Asclepias Asthmatica. (W) *Automel* H.(2)
Asclepias Vomitoria. Kœnig's Ms.

I have inserted this plant on the authority of the following note, which was found among the late Dr. Kœnig's papers, and communicated to me by Dr. Roxburgh. "Dr. Patrick Russell was "informed by the Physician-General at *Madras,* "that he had, many years before, known it (the "root of the *Asclepias Vomitoria)* used, both by "the *European* and native troops, with great suc"cess, in the dysentery, which happened at that "time to be epidemic in the camp. The store of "ipecacuanha, had, it seems, been wholly expend"ed ; and Dr. Anderson, finding the practice of

(1) *Isarmul.* (2) *Uotomul.*

"the black doctors much more successful than his "own, was not ashamed to take instruction from "them, which he pursued with good success; and "collecting a quantity of the plant which they "pointed out to him, he sent a large package of the "roots to *Madras*. It is certainly an article of "the Materia Medica highly deserving attention."

I have not obtained any further account of the medicinal virtues of this species of *Asclepias*, which grows in the *Northern Circars*; but is not met with in *Bengal*. It is, however, as Dr. KŒNIG observes, an article highly deserving attention. The ipecacuanha root is one of the few medicines for which we have not as yet found any adequate substitute in *India*; and, if such a substitute should be found in the root of the *Asclepias Asthmatica*, it would prove a most valuable acquisition to our Materia Medica.

BOSWELLIA SERRATA. (ROXB.) *Salai* H. *Sallaci* S.
LIBANUS THURIFERA. (COLEBROOKE.)
Olibanum (The Gum-resin) { *Cundur*(1) and *Gendeh firozeh*,(2) H. *Cundura* S.
As. Res. IX. 377.

The grateful odour diffused by Olibanum, when thrown on the fire, must have early attracted the notice of mankind, as it appears that this fragrant gum-resin was used as incense, in the religious ce-

(1) *Coondoor*. (2) *Gundu-feerozu* or *Gundu-birozu*.

remonies of almost all the antient nations. Of this honour it has kept possession, from the most remote antiquity, until the present time, when (unless when its place is supplied by *Benzoin,)* it still continues to perfume the churches, mosques and temples, both in *Europe* and *Asia.*

That naturalists should have remained in ignorance or in errour, until almost the present day, respecting the tree which yields a substance so long known, and so universally used, must appear not a little surprising. Such, however, is the fact; and the merit of having discovered the true origin of this celebrated incense, is due to Mr. Colebrooke, who has ascertained and proved, most satisfactorily, that the olibanum, or frankincense of the antients, is not the gum-resin of the *Juniperus Lycia,* as was generally supposed, but the produce of our *Libanus Thurifera.* See his paper on this subject, in the Asiatick Researches, Vol. IX. p. 377, to which is subjoined a botanical description of the tree by Dr. Roxburgh.

Although the olibanum is still retained in the pharmacopœias of the three *British* colleges, it is seldom used as a medicine in modern practice. Formerly, however, it was held in considerable estimation, as a remedy in catarrh and hœmoptysis; and as it is less heating than myrrh, by which it has been superseded in these diseases, it might still, perhaps, be used with advantage, in some cases, in which the myrrh might prove too stimulant.

Cæsalpinia Bonducella. (W.) *Catcaranja*(1) *Cat-caléjí*(2) [H. *Puti-Caranja* S.

This shrub is a native of both the *Indies;* but its use in medicine is, I believe, known only in the *East*. The kernels of the seeds are intensely bitter, and possess the tonic power in a very high degree. They are accordingly employed by the *Hindu* physicians, in all cases in which that power is more especially required; and particularly in intermittent fevers, for which they are considered as an almost infallible remedy. The mode of using them is as follows. One of the seeds, freed from its hard shell, is beat into a paste, with a few drops of water, and three corns of black pepper. This is formed into three pills, which are taken for a dose, and this dose is repeated, three or four times a day; or oftener if necessary. The decoction of the *Gentiana Cherayita* (Roxb.) is generally prescribed, to be taken at the same time with the pills. See *Gentiana Cherayita.*

This method of curing intermittents is so generally successful, that it has been adopted by many *European* practitioners; particularly in those cases, which so frequently occur, in which the patients have an aversion to the *Peruvian* bark, or cannot

(1) *Kut-kurunja.* (2) *Kut-kuléea.*

retain it on the stomach. In all such cases, and also on occasions where the *Peruvian* bark cannot be procured, I believe that the *Catcaranja* will be found one of the best substitutes to which we can have recourse; particularly if assisted by the decoction of the *Cherayita,* which indeed is so powerful an auxiliary, that it may be doubtful, in the case of success, to which of the two remedies the cure should be chiefly ascribed.

Cannabis Sativa. (W.) *B'hang* and *Gánja* H. *Ganjicá* S.
Murray, IV. 608.

Lamarck is of opinion that the *Indian Gánja* is a different species of *Cannabis* from the *Cannabis Sativa,* and names it "*Cannabis Indica foliis alternis.*" (Encyc. Bot. I. 695.) But Willdenow, after remarking that the *European* species has also alternate leaves, assures us that on comparing it with many specimens of the *Indian* plant, he could not perceive any difference between them; See Sp. Pl. IV. 763. neither could Dr. Roxburgh, on comparing plants raised from *Europe* hemp-seed with the *Gánja* plant, discover in the latter the slightest distinction; not even enough on which to found a variety.

Capsicum Frutescens. (W.) *Lál Mirch* H.

Capsicum Annuum. { Murray, I. 732. / Woodville, III. 391. }

The annual species of *Capsicum* is not a native of this country, and but rarely found in the gardens. The *Capsicum frutescens*, of which there are several varieties, is cultivated in every part of *India*, on account of its pods; which afford to the inhabitants a condiment, as necessary for their rice and pulse diet, as salt itself. In respect to the medical uses of this species, they perfectly correspond with those of the *Capsicum annuum*, for which see the authors above referred to.

CARICA PAPAYA. (W.) *Papuiya* H.(1) RUMP. *Amb.* I. [Tab. 50. 51.

This is not an indigenous tree of *India*, and consequently has no name in the *Sanscrit* language. It is a native of *South-America* and the *West-Indies*; whence it was brought, by the *Spaniards* and *Portuguese*, to the *Philippines* and *Moluccas*; and from these islands, being of very quick growth, it spread rapidly to all the other countries of *India*. It has long been cultivated in every quarter of *Hindustàn*, and is in flower and fruit during the greatest part of the year. The milky juice, that flows from the fruit, when an incision is made into it, before it is quite ripe, is esteemed, by the inhabitants of the *Isle of France* and *Bourbon*, as the most powerful vermifuge that has yet been discovered. An account of this remedy was transmitted to the President of the Asiatick Society, by Mr. CHARPENTIER COSSIGNI, in a letter, dated

(1). *Papueya.*

the 3d November 1800, of which the following is an extract.

" Un hazard heureux a fait decouvrir a *L'Isle* " *de la Reunion* un remede le plus efficace de tous " ceux connus contre les vers. Il y a plusieurs an- " nées qu'on en fait usage avec le plus grand suc- " cés, *a L'Isle de France,* ou les maladies vermi- " neuses sont tres communes. C'est du lait de " papayes. On incise ce fruit quand il est verd. " Il rend un lait, qu'on recueille, et qu'on fait " prendre á jeun au malade. C'est le plus puissant " de tous le vermifuges. On pretend qu'il tue " meme le Tænia cucurbìteux, qui est assez com- " mun dans *L'Isle.* Au reste, les preuves de la " vertu puissante de ce remede sont deja tres nom- " breuses, sans qu'il soit resulté d'accidens, quoìqu' " on ait essayé de l'administrer en grande dose. Ce " qui rend ce remede precieux, c'est qu'une seule " dose suffit pour tuer tous les vers, quelle grande " qu'en soit la quantité."

The vermifage, thus strongly recommended, and on such respectable authority, has not yet come into use here, either among the native or *European* practitioners; although an account of it was published, at the time, in the *Calcutta* newspapers. A remedy, however, so simple, and so easily at all times to be procured, certainly deserves to have a fair trial. The dose for an infant is one tea spoonful of the juice, mixed with thrice that quantity of warm water, or cow's milk; for a child of six or seven years of age, one table spoonful; and, for an adult, two table spoonfuls. A few hours after the patient has taken the dose of *Papaya* milk, a dose of *Oleum Ricini* is given to him, to promote the expulsion of the dead worms.

CASSIA FISTULA. (W.) *Ameltás*(1) H. *Suvernaca* S.
MURRAY, II. 510.
WOODVILLE, III. 449.

CASSIA ALATA. (W.) *Dád-merden*(2) H. *Dádrughna* S.

This shrub grows wild in various parts of *Hindustàn* and is cultivated, in *Bengal,* as an ornament to the flower-garden. The expressed juice of the leaves, mixed with common salt, is used externally, for curing the ring-worms. From this quality, it has obtained its *Hindustàni* and *Sanscrit* names; and, for the same reason, it is called, by RUMPHIUS, *Herpetica;* and, by *French* authors, *Herbe á Dartres.* Notwithstanding this general prepossession in its favour, in the many trials which I have made of it, for curing herpetic eruptions, I have oftener failed than succeeded.

CEDRELA TUNA. (W.) *Tún*(3) H. *Tunna* and *Cuvéraca* S. [*Suren Malay*, *Surenus*. RUMPH. *Hort. Amb.* III. 68. Tab. 39.

See a botanical description of this tree by Sir

(1) *Umultas.* (2) *Dad murdun.* (3) *Toon.*

WILLIAM JONES, in the 4th Vol. of the As. Res, p. 273. The wood is esteemed on account of its close grain, and beautiful colour, resembling that of mahogany, and is much employed, by the cabinet-makers in *Calcutta*, for the purpose of being made into furniture. No part of the tree is used in medicine by the *Hindus*; but a very intelligent *English* surgeon, now deceased, found the powder of the bark, and the extract made from it, very efficacious in the cure of fevers. He also experienced great advantage from the powder, applied externally, in the treatment of different kinds of ulcers. See a letter to Dr. DUNCAN, from Mr. J. KENNEDY, surgeon at *Chunar*. (Annals of Medicine I. 387.)

* I have not met with any other account of the medicinal qualities of the *Tún* bark; but, on so respectable authority, I judged it a proper object of further inquiry, and have therefore given the tree a place in the catalogue.

CITRUS AURANTIUM. (W.) *Narenj*(1) and *Narengi* (the smallest) *Narango* S.
Coula(2) (the common sort)
Santara(3) (the China orange)

CITRUS MEDICA. (W.) *Lému*(4) H. *Jambíra* S.
MURRAY, III. 265. 284.
WOODVILLE, III. 496. 500.

* I have since found in RUMPHIUS, that an infusion of the bark and leaves of this tree, with the addition of the root of the *Acorus Calamus*, is highly esteemed by the *Javanese* as a remedy in fevers, and that the *Residuum* of the infusion, made into a liniment with vinegar, is used by them externally as a discutient in obstructions and indurations of the spleen (*vide loc. Citat.*)

(1) *Narunj and Narungee.* (2) *Kuola.* (3) *Sungtura.* (4) *Lemee.*

Cordia Myxa. (W.) *Lehsóra*(1) H. *Bahuváraca* S.
MURRAY, II. 133.
WOODVILLE, IV. 16.

Coriandrum Sativum. (W.) *D'hanya*(2) H. *D'hanyáca* S.
MURRAY, I. 405
WOODVILLE, III. 492.

Croton Tiglium. (W.) *Jeypál* & *Jemálgóta*(3) H. *Jayapála* S.
MURRAY, IV. 149.
RUMPH. AMB, IV. Tab. 42.

The seeds of this plant were formerly well known in *Europe*, under the names of *Grana Tiglia*, and *Grana Molucca*. They were employed as hydragogue purgatives; but, on account of the violence of their operation, they have been long banished from modern practice. For the same reason, they are seldom used by the *Hindu* practitioners, though not unfrequently taken, as purgatives, by the poorer classes of the natives. One seed is sufficient for a dose. It is first carefully cleared from the membranaceous parts, (the rudiments of the seminal leaves,) that adhere to the centre of it; by which precaution, it is found to act less roughly; and then rubbed with a little rice gruel, or with a bit of the plantain fruit.

Cucumis Colocynthis. (W.) *Indráini*(4) H. *Indravárini* S.
MURRAY, I. 583.
WOODVILLE, III. 476.

Cuminum Cyminum. (W.) *Jírá*(5) H. *Jiraca* S.
MURRAY, I. 391.
WOODVILLE, III. 521.

---

(1) *Luhsora.* (2) *D'hunya.* (3) *Jumalgota.* (4) *Indrayun.* (5) *Jeera.*

Curcuma Longa. (W.) *Haldí*(1) H. *Haridrá* S.
Murray, V. 73.
Woodville, II. 359.

Curcuma Zedoaria. (Roxb. MS.) *Nirbisí*(2) H. *Nirbisha* S.
Amomum Zedoaria. (W.)

Kæmpferia Rotunda. { Murray, V. 82. Woodville, II. 361.

Sp. Ch.—Spikes lateral. Bulbs small, with long yellow palmated tubers. Leaves broad, lanceolar, subsessile on their sheath. Sericeous underneath. Colour, uniform green. (Roxb. MS.)

From the roots of several species of *Curcuma*, that are found in *Bengal*, the natives prepare a farinaceous powder, which they call *Tikhur*.(3) It is in every respect similar to the power prepared from the root of the *Maranta Arundinacea*, or arrow-root; and is often sold for it in the *Calcutta* shops.

Datura Metel. (W.) *D'hatúra*(4) H. *D'hustúra* S.

For *Datura Stramonium* See { Murray, I. 670. Woodville, II. 338.

The *D. Stramonium*, which is the species used in medicine in *Europe*, is not found in *Hindustan*,* but the *D. Metel* grows wild in every part of the country. The soporiferous and intoxicating qualities of the seeds are well known to the inhabitants; and it appears, from the records of the

(1) *Huldee.* (2) *Nirbissee.* (3) *Teekhoor.* (4) *D'hutooru.*

* In the Asiatic Researches, VI. 351. Colonel Hardwicke, enumerates the *Datura Stramonium* among the plants which he found in the *Sirinagur* country; but he afterwards ascertained, that the plant which he met with, was the *Datura Metel*; and has candidly authorized me to notice the mistake.

native courts of justice, that these seeds are still frequently employed, for the same licentious and wicked purposes, as they were formerly, in the time of ACOSTA and RUMPHIUS. (See RUMPH. *Amb.* V. 242.) I do not know that either the seeds or the extract prepared from the expressed juice of the plant, are used in medicine here; but those who place any faith in the accounts given by Baron STOERCK, and Mr. ODHELIUS* of the efficacy of the extract of the *Stramonium,* in the cure of mania, epilepsy, and other convulsive disorders, may reasonably expect the same effects from the extract of the *Metel;* the narcotic power in the two species being perfectly alike. LINNÆUS, indeed, has given a place, in his *Materia Medica,* to the *Metel,* in preference to the *Stramonium.*

DATURA FASTUOSA. (W.) *Lal D'hatúra* H.

This species is cultivated in gardens, and makes a fine appearance with its tall red polished stalk, and beautiful purple flowers. It is also found growing wild on commons, and amidst the rubbish of ruined buildings. I have inserted it in the catalogue in consequence of having been favoured by Dr. HUNTER, with the following communication.

" The *Datura Fastuosa,* is employed in *Ceylon,* " as a remedy for *Spasmodic Asthma.* The part

---

* Vide MURRAY & WOODVILLE, loc. citat.

" used is the root, which is dried in the shade, " beaten so as to make the fibres separate, and " then cut into small pieces to be smoked in a " common tobacco pipe. One or two pipefuls " may be smoked when the fit is expected, or even " after its accession, when it seldom fails to relieve " it; occasioning some heat in the chest, followed " by expectoration. It in general also produces " giddiness, followed by drowsiness and inclina- " tion to sleep. The *Datura Fastuosa*, is com- " monly cultivated in the gardens about *Columbo*, " but I understand that the *Datura Metel*, which " grows in great abundance in this neighbour- " hood, possesses similar virtues."

Extract of a Letter from THOMAS CRISTIE, ESQ. *to* DR. WILLIAM HUNTER; *dated 3d Feb.* 1810.

DAUCUS CAROTA. (W.) *Gajer*(1) H. *Garjara* S.
MURRAY, I. 316.
WOODVILLE, III. 443.

DOLICHOS PRURIENS. (W.) *Kiwách* H. *Capicach'hu* S.
MURRAY, II. 438.
WOODVILLE, III. 468.

ECHITES ANTIDYSENTERICA. (ROXB. MS.) *Curayia*(2) H. [*Cutaja* S.

The seed, *Inderjao* H. *Indrayava* S.

Nerium Antidysentericum. { MURRAY, I. 828. WOODVILLE, IV. 42. }

EUPATORIUM AYAPANA. (W.)

This plant was brought, about ten years ago, from *Brazil*, of which country it is a native, to the *Isle of France*; and was, by the islanders,

(1) *Gajur.* (2) *Kooraya.*

considered for a time, as almost a panacea. It appears, however, that it has entirely lost its credit with them, and that they do not now allow it to possess any medicinal virtue whatsoever. See BORY DE ST. VINCENT, *voyage aux principales Isles des Mers d' Afrique*. The instances are not unfrequent, of medicines which had been at first too highly extolled, having afterwards met with unmerited neglect; and such may, perhaps, be the case, in respect to the plant in question; which has been lately introduced into *Bengal*, and is now cultivated in the gardens about *Calcutta*. I have therefore inserted the *Ayapana* in the catalogue, as an object deserving further inquiry. Its congener, the *Eupatorium Cannabinum*, was strongly recommended by TOURNEFORT and CHOMEL, as a deobstruent, in visceral obstructions consequent to intermittent fevers; and externally, as a discutient, in hydropic swellings of the legs and scrotum. See MURRAY, I. 202.

GENTIANA CHIRAYITA. (ROXB. MS.) *Chiráyita* H. *Cirátaticta* S.

Sp. Ch.—Herbaceous. Leaves stem-clasping, lanceolate. 3—5 nerved. Corol rotate, four cleft, smooth. Stamens four. Capsule ovate, bifurcate, as long as the calyx. (ROXB. MS.)

This species of *Gentian* is indigenous in the mountainous countries to the northward of the *Ganges*; but does not grow in the lower parts of *Bengal*. The dried herb, however, is to be met with in every bazar of *Hindustan*, being a medicine in the highest repute, with both the *Hindu* and *European* practitioners. It possesses all the stomachic, tonic, febrifuge and antarthritic virtues, which are ascribed to the *Gentiana Lutea*, and in a greater degree than they are generally found in that root, in the state in which it comes to us from *Europe*. It may therefore, on every occasion, be advantageously substituted for it. The efficacy of the *Chirayita*, when combined with the *Caranja* nut, in curing intermittents, has been already mentioned. It is found equally powerful in exciting and strengthening the action of the stomach, and obviating flatulency, acidity and redundancy of phlegm, in dyspepsia and gout. For restoring the tone and activity of the moving fibre, in general debility, and in that kind of cachexy which is liable to terminate in dropsy, the *Chirayita* will be found one of the most useful and effectual remedies which we can employ.

The parts of the plant that are used in medicine, are the dried stalks, with pieces of the root adhering to them. A decoction of these, or which is better, an infusion of them in hot water, is the form usually administered. Spirituous tinctures are also prepared from the plant, with the addition of orange-peel and cardamom seeds; and those who consider such tinctures as of any avail, will find these very agreeable *bitters*. The most useful purpose, however, to which the tincture can be applied, is that of being added to the decoction, or infusion, with the view of rendering them more grateful to the stomach.

Glycyrrhiza Glabra. (W.) *Jét'himad'h*(1) H. *Yastimadhuca* S.

Murray, II. 457.
Woodville, III. 458.

Hyperanthera Moringa. (W.) *Sahijana*(2) H. *Sóbhanjana* S.

Guilandina Moringa. Murray, II. 521.

This tree, on account of its beauty, as well as its utility, is a favourite with the natives of *Hindustan*, who are fond of planting it near their houses, both in the towns and villages. The *Legumes*, blossoms and leaves are all esculent, and are used both as pot-herbs and for pickles. The root of the young tree, when scraped, so exactly resembles horse-radish, as scarcely to be distinguished from it by the nicest palate; and is therefore used, by *Europeans*, instead of that root, as a condiment with animal food. In medicine, it completely supplies its place, whether employed externally, as a rubefacient, or used as a stimulant internally, in cases of palsy, chronic rheumatism and dropsy. The expressed oil of the seeds is employed externally, for relieving the pain of the joints, in gout and acute rheumatism. This oil is remarkable for re-

(1) *Jet'heemud'h.* (2) *Suhujna.*

sisting rancidity, and, on that account, has been selected by the perfumers, as the fittest for being impregnated with the odor of jessamines, violets, tuberoses and other flowers which yield little or no essential oil, but impart their fragrance to expressed oils.

The seeds of this tree are the *Ben nuts* of the old writers on pharmacy. Some of these writers supposed their *Lignum Nephriticum* to be the wood of the *Moringa,* but erroneously, the tree which affords that wood being a native of *New Spain.*

Jatropha Curcas. (W.) *Bágbarindá* H.
Murray, IV. 164.

The seeds of this plant, like those of the *Croton Tiglium,* (to which it is nearly allied,) are frequently used as a purgative, by the more indigent natives. Their operation is milder than that of the *Tiglium* seeds, and two or three may be taken for a dose; but the same precaution must be used, in freeing them from the membranaceous parts, that was formerly directed to be observed in respect to the *Tiglium* seeds.

Justicia Paniculata. (W.) *Calapnát'h*(1) and *Crëat* H.
[*Cairáta* S.

This species of *Justicia* is a native of *Bengal,* and of many other parts of *Hindustàn.* The whole

(1) *Kulupnat'h.*

of the plant is intensely bitter, and it yields this quality equally to aqueous, vinous and spirituous menstrua. It is much used, by the native practitioners, in fevers and dysenteries. The *French* and *Portuguese* inhabitants of *India* consider it as an excellent stomachic; and it forms the basis of their bitter tincture, so well known, on the *Malabar* coast, by the name of *Drogue Amere*.

LAURUS CINNAMOMUM. (W.) *Dárchinì*(1) H. *Dárasita* S.
MURRAY, IV. 417.
WOODVILLE, I. 80.

LAURUS CASSIA. (W.) *Tej pát* H. *Tamála patrá* S.
The Bark *Tej*(2) H. *Twacha* S.
MURRAY, IV. 441.
WOODVILLE, I. 82.

LIGUSTICUM AJAWAIN. (ROXB. MS.) *Ajawain*(3) H. *Yavání* S.

Sp. Ch.—Annual. Erect. Leaves superdecompound with filiform leaflets. Ridges and furrows of the seeds distinct and scabrous.

The seed of this species of lovage is an excellent aromatic. It is much used by the natives as an agreeable condiment in their dishes, and for improving the flavour of the betel leaf and nut in their *Páns*. In medicine, it is esteemed a powerful remedy in the flatulent colic; and is employed by the veterinary practitioners in analogous diseases of horses and cows.

---

(1) *Darcheenee.* (2) *Tuj.* (3) *Ujwayun.*

This is the seed mentioned and recommended to notice by the late Dr. PERCIVAL, in his Essays, (I. 433.) under the name of *Ajava* seed.

LINUM USITATISSIMUM. (W.) *Tisí*(1) H. *Atasi* S.
MURRAY, III. 474.
WOODVILLE, II. 303.

MELIA AZEDIRACHTA. (W.) *Nimb*(2) H. *Nimba* S.
MELIA SEMPERVIRENS. (W.) *Bacäin*(3) H. *Mahá-Nimba* S.

These two species of the bead-tree, are small elegant trees, cultivated very generally in *Hindustàn*, on account of their beautiful blossoms, and the medicinal qualities of the leaves. The leaves have a nauseous, bitter taste, (devoid of astringency) which they readily impart to water. The decoction of them is used internally, in cases in which the tonic and stomachic virtues of simple Bitters are required. They are also employed, externally, as discutients and emollients, either in fomentations, or in the form of cataplasm; for which last purpose they are simply heated in an earthen pot, and then bruised and applied to the part affected.

MENISPERMUM CORDIFOLIUM. (W.) *Gurcha*(4) H. *Guduchi* S.
Cit-amerdu. VAN RHEEDE, H. M. VII. 39.
MENISPERMUM VERRUCOSUM. (ROXB. Ms.) *Putra Waly* Javanese.
Funis felleus. RUMPH. *Amb.* V. 82.

Sp. Ch.—Perennial. Scandent. Verrucose. Leaves cordate, acuminate, entire, smooth. Male racemes from the naked branches, simple. Nectareal scales inserted in the filaments.

(1) *Teesee.* (2) *Neemb.* (3) *Bukayun.* (4) *Goorcha.*

The *Menispermum Cordifolium* is indigenous in most parts of *Hindustàn*. The decoction of the leaves is prescribed by the *Hindu* physicians, as a febrifuge, and as a tonic in gout. It is also one of the many remedies which they give for the cure of jaundice. The very young leaves are employed externally, as an emollient, made into the form of liniment, with milk.

The *Menispermum Verrucosum* was introduced into *Bengal*, from *Malacca*, by Captain WRIGHT, about ten years ago; and is now cultivated in the gardens about *Calcutta*. It is readily propagated from cuttings, which are remarkable for the great length of time during which they preserve the power of vegetation. Every part of the plant is exceedingly bitter, particularly the stalk; which, from this quality, has obtained its *Javanese* name, *Putrà Wali;* literally translated by RUMPHIUS, *funis felleus*. It is the remedy generally employed, in the *Malay* countries, for the cure of intermittent fevers; and, from Captain WRIGHT's account, is as powerful a febrifuge as the *Peruvian* bark. It has not, however, come into use here; nor, while we have other approved remedies, is there any occasion for having recourse to it; but I have given it a place in the catalogue, for the sake of captains and surgeons of ships, trading to the eastward, who, should their stock of bark at any time fail them, may, in all the *Malay* islands, find a valuable substitute for it in the *Purra Wali.*

Mentha Sativa. (W.) *Podina*(1) H.
Mentha Crispa. Murray, II. 178.
Mentha viridis. Woodville, III. 463.

The mint so generally used in *Bengal,* both for medicinal and culinary purposes is a different plant from the *Spear mint* (*Méntha viridis* W.) but I have not been able to ascertain to what species it ought to be referred. Dr. Roxburgh is of opinion that, if it be not the same, it comes nearest to the *Mentha Sativa* (W.) In a medical view, this uncertainty is not of much importance, as our *Podina* possesses fully the aromatic flavour, as well as the stomachic, antispasmodic and emmenagogue virtues, which seem common to most of the species of this genus.

Mirabilis Jalappa. (W.) *Gûl Abbas* H.

This is not an indigenous plant of *Hindustan;* but all the beautiful varieties of it are now cultivated, as an ornament to the gardens in *Bengal.*

The official jalap was formerly supposed to be the root of this species of *Mirabilis;* and hence it obtained its trivial name; but that valuable drug is now ascertained to be the root of a species of *Convolvulus.* As the *Mirabilis,* however, had so long retained the credit of affording the jalap;

(1) *Poodeena.*

and, with authors of the highest authority in botany, from PLUMIER to LINNÆUS, I was desirous of discovering what degree of purgative quality it really possessed. With that view, having carefully dried and powdered some of the root, I sent it, for trial, to the *European* and native hospitals. Dr. HUNTER's report, from the former of these, is as follows: "We have tried the *Mirabilis* with "thirteen patients. They do not complain of its "being disagreeable to the taste, nor of its exciting "nausea or griping; but its operation, as a purge, "is uncertain, and two drams of it sometimes pro-"cure only a single stool. It seemed to answer "best with those who had bowel complaints." Dr. SHOOLBRED found the root equally weak and uncertain in its operation, in the trials which he made of it, in the native hospital.

NICOTIANA TABACUM. (W.) *Tambácu*(1) H. *Támracuta* S.
MURRAY, I. 670.
WOODVILLE, II. 338.

NIGELLA INDICA. (ROXB. MS.) *Cálá Jíra*(2) H. *Musaví* S.

Sp. Ch.—Annual. Petals entire. Pistils five: length of the stamina. Leaves decompound. Exterior lip of the nectary ovate, and deeply two cleft. Interior entire and acute. (ROXB. MS.)

The seed of this plant is used by the natives more in diet than in medicine; and, on account of its agreeable flavour and taste, forms the principal

(1) *Tumbakoo.* (2) *Kalajeera.*

condiment in the *Curries*. The seed of its congener, the *Nigella Sativa*, is, in like manner, the favourite spice of some nations on the continent of *Europe;* particularly the *Hanoverians*, who have given it the name of *tout epice*. See MURRAY, III. 34, and PLENCK, Plant. Med. V. 49.

OCIMUM PILOSUM. (ROXB. MS.) *Rihán* H.
The seed, *Tukhmi Rihán*(1) H.

Sp. Ch.—Shrubby. Hairy. Branches four sided. Leaves ovate, oblong, serrated, with margins and petioles hairy. Bracts petioled, ovate, cordate, ciliate. Upper lip of the calyx round, cordate and hairy; with corol twice its length. (ROXB. MS.)

Many species of the *Ocimum* are common in *Bengal*, and comprehended under the generic name of *Tulasi*. One of them, the *Ocimum Sanctum*, (W.)? *Parnasa* in *Sanscrit*, is well known to be held in higher veneration, by the *Hindus*, than any other plant. See As. Res. IV. 280. The leaves of most of the species have a slightly aromatic taste, and a strong, but not disagreeable smell.

I have given the *Rìhán* a place in the catalogue, on account of the peculiar quality of its seed, which, when infused in cold water, forms a mucilage much used by the natives as a demulcent in catarrhs. From the slight aroma which it possesses, it lies easier on the stomach than most other vegetable mucilages. It is a favourite medicine

(1) *Tookhmi rihan.*

with the native women, who take it after parturition, and suppose that it relieves the after-pains.

Papaver Somniferum. (W.) *Post* H. *C'hasa* S.
Opium, *Afiùn* H. & Pers.
Murray, II. 254.
Woodville, III. 503.

Phyllanthus Emblica. (W.) *Aonla*(1) H. *Amalaci* S.
Murray, IV. 127.

This tree is found, both in a wild and cultivated state, in most parts of *Hindustàn*. Its fruit is one of those which were formerly known in *Europe* under the name of *Myrobalans,* but which have been long discarded from the pharmacopœias. It is, however, in general use with the *Hindu* physicians, as an eccoprotic, and enters into many of their compositions. It is particularly an essential ingredient in the preparation of the *Bitlaban,* a medicinal salt which will be afterwards noticed.

Piper Nigrum. (W.) *Mirch* H. *Maricha* S.
Murray, V. 22.
Woodville, III. 513.

Piper Longum. (W.) *Pipel*(2) H. *Pippali* S.
Murray, V. 35.
Woodville, III. 516.

Plantago Ispaghul. (Roxb. MS.) *Ispaghul*(3) H.

Sp. Ch.—Caulescent. Leaves linear, lanceolate, three nerved, slightly wooly. Peduncles axillary. Head cylindric. Capsule two-seeded. (Roxb. MS.)

This plant was formerly supposed to be the

---

(1) *Uonla & Awula.* (2) *Peepul.* (3) *Ispughool.*

Plantago Psyllium (L.) but is certainly a different species. It is cultivated in *Bengal,* on account of the seeds, which, like those of the *P. Psyllium,* form a rich mucilage with boiling water. For this purpose, a pint of water is poured on about two drams of the seeds. This mucilage is very generally used, as a demulcent, in catarrhs, nephritic pains, heat of urine, and other diseases in which acrimony is to be obviated or palliated.

PLUMBAGO ZEYLANICA. (W.) *Chít'a*(1) H. *Chitraca* S.
PLUMBAGO ROSEA. (W.) *Lál Chít'a* H. *Racta Chitraca* S.

Both these shrubs are cultivated in *Bengal* as flower plants. Every part of them is extremely acrid, particularly the root; which, in its recent state, being bruised, is employed, by the *Hindu* practitioners, as a vesicatory.

The *Plumbago Europæa* is mentioned by MURRAY (I. 772.) as having been found efficacious in the cure of cancer, for which purpose the ulcers are dressed, thrice a day, with olive oil, in which the leaves of the plant have been infused. The authorities which he quotes, for the cures effected by this application, are respectable; and, as our species coincide entirely in quality with the *Plumbago Europæa,* it may be worth while to make a trial of their power, in a disease so deplorable, for which no adequate remedy has yet been discovered.

---

(1) *Cheeta.*

Pterocarpus Santalinus. (W.) *Ract Chandan*(1) H.
[*Racta Chandana* S.
Murray, VI. 59.
Woodville, IV. 109.

Punica Granatum. (W.) *Anár* H. *Dadima* S.
Murray, III. 262.
Woodville, I. 158.

The flowers of this beautiful shrub, which were formerly well known under the name of *Balaustines*, are now neglected; but the rind of the fruit is still considered as one of the most useful medicinal astringents, in cases wherein that quality, simply, is required. This shrub affords another valuable remedy, in the fresh bark of its root, for the knowledge of which we are indebted to the *Hindu* physicians. See " an account of an *Indian* " remedy for the tape-worm," by Dr. Buchanan, in the *Edinburgh* Medical and Chirurgical Journal, No. IX. p. 22.

The *Tœnia* is not a common disorder in *Bengal;* but, since the date of Dr. Buchanan's communication, several cases of it have occurred here to Dr. Hunter, and to Dr Shoolbred, in which the bark of the pomegranate root was used with complete success, and without having failed in a single instance.* The following is the method in which it is prepared and administered. Eight ounces of the fresh bark of the root are boiled, in three pints

(1) *Rukut Chundun.*

* See some additional proofs of its efficacy in the Appendix.

of water, to a quart. Of this decoction, the patient takes a wine-glass-full; and repeats that quantity, at longer or shorter intervals, as the sickness and faintness, which it generally occasions, will allow; until he has taken the whole. The worm is commonly voided, in a few hours after the patient has begun to take the medicine; and, not unfrequently, comes away alive.

Ricinus Communis. (W.) *Arend*(1) H. *E'randa* S.

This plant is cultivated, for both œconomical and medicinal purposes, over all *Hindustàn*. The expressed oil of the seeds, so well known in *Europe*, under the name of *castor oil*, is more generally used, as a purgative, than any other medicine; and perhaps there is no other, on which we may, with so much confidence, rely, as a safe, and, at the same time, an active cathartic. It may be given, with propriety, in every case in which that class of remedies is required, (unless when the most drastic are necessary,) and to patients of every age and constitution; for though it seldom fails to produce the effect intended, it operates without heat or irritation.

The oil should be expressed, in the manner directed by the *London* College, from the decorticated seeds, and without the assistance of heat. That which is obtained by boiling the seeds in

---

(1) *Urund.*

water, is injured both in smell and taste, and becomes sooner rancid than the oil procured by expression.

Rubia Manjit'h. (Roxb. MS.) *Manjít'h*(1) H. *Manjist'há* S.

Sp. Ch.—Pentandrous. Perennial. Scandent. Branches with four hispid angles. Leaves quatern, long-petioled, cordate, acuminate, 5—7 nerved. Hispid. (Roxb. Ms.)

This species of madder is indigenous in *Nepal*, and is used by the dyers and calico-printers, in the same manner as the *Rubia Tinctorum* is in *Europe*. Parcels of it have been frequently sent to *England*, where it was found equal in quality to the best *Dutch* madder. I know not that it has ever been tried here in medicine; but, from its sensible qualities being the same with those of the *Rubia Tinctorum*, there is reason to conclude that it may be found equally efficacious with that drug, as a deobstruent and emmenagogue. See Murray, I. 523. Woodville, II. 190.

Ruta Graveolens. (W.) *Saturi* H.
Murray, III. 112.
Woodville, I. 108.

Santalum Album. (W.) *Chandan*(2) H. *Chahdane* S.
Murray, II. 114.
Woodville, IV. 136.

Sida Cordifolia. (W.) *Barïála*(3) H. *Bat'yâluca* S.

Sida Rhombifolia (W.) *Lál Barïála* H.

Sida Rhomboidœa. (Roxb. Ms.) *Saféd Barïála*, H.

Sp. Ch.—Shrubby. Erect. Ramous. Leaves short-petioled, rhomboid, lanceolate, serrate, 3-nerved, villous. Stf.

(1) *Munjeet'h.* (2) *Chundun.* (3) *Buryala.*

pules setaceous. Peduncles axillary, solitary, shorter than the leaves, one-flowered. Capsules 10, without beak. (ROXB. MS.)

There are several other species of the *Sida* in *Bengal*; but I have selected these three, as being the kinds most generally used in medicine by the *Hindus*. Like the other columniferous plants, they all abound in mucilage, and are much employed by the natives as demulcents and emollients. They possess these virtues, in at least an equal degree with our officinal *Althœa* and *Malva*; and may well supply their place, either for internal use, or, externally, for fomentations, cataplasms and enemata. See MURRAY, III. 357. WOODVILLE, I. 146.

SINAPIS DICHOTOMA. (ROXB. MS.) *Serson*,(1) H. *Sarshapa*, S.

Sp. Ch.—Dichotomous. Siliques cylindric, smooth, spreading. Beak straight and tapering. Leaves stem-clasping; the lower somewhat lyred. Superiour ovate, lanceolate, entire. All are smooth, as are also the stem and branches.

[ROXB. MS.

SINAPIS RAMOSA. (ROXB. MS.) *Raï*,(2) H. *Rájicá*, S.

Sp. Ch.—Annual. Erect. Ramous. Siliques expanding, linear, vertically compressed, smooth. Leaves petioled; lower lyred: superiour sublanceolate. (ROXB. MS.)

Both these species of mustard, as well as a third species called *Torí*(3) H. *Tuvericá*, S. are extensively cultivated in *Bengal*, on account of the oil procured from the seeds. In respect to medicinal qualities, these seeds correspond exactly with the

(1) *Surson.* (2) *Raee.* (3) *Toree.*

seed of the *Sinapis Nigra,* (W.) and may be used, with equal advantage, as the latter, either internally, as stimulants in rheumatic and paralytic affections, or externally for sinapisms. See MURRAY, II. 398. WOODVILLE, III. 409.

STRYCHNOS NUX VOMICA. (W.) *Cuchila*(1) H. *Culaca* S.
MURRAY, I. 703.
WOODVILLE, IV. 29.
STRYCHNOS POTATORUM. (W.) *Nir-malli*(2) H. *Cataca* S.

The seeds of the *Strychnos Nux Vomica* are reckoned amongst the most powerful of the narcotic poisons. In *Germany,* nevertheless, they are considered as *medicinal,* and have been recommended, by many authors of that nation, as efficacious antispasmodics and tonics; but the *British* physicians have prudently abstained from the use of so dangerous a remedy; and, for the same reason, these seeds are seldom, if ever, employed in medicine by the *Hindus.* They are sometimes used, however, for a very pernicious purpose, by the distillers, who add a quantity of them in the process of distilling arrack, to render the spirit more intoxicating.

The seeds of the *Strychnos Potatorum,* though never used in medicine, are highly valuable, to both *Europeans* and natives, from the quality which they possess, of clearing muddy water, and

(1) *Koochila.* (2) *Nirmullee.*

rendering it potable; to which the trivial name of the tree, first given to it by KŒNIG, alludes. One of the seeds is rubbed very hard, for a minute or two, round the inside of an earthen vessel, into which the water is poured and left to settle. In a short time, the impurities subside, and leave the water perfectly limpid and tasteless.

SWIETENIA FEBRIFUGA. (W.) *Rohuna* H. *Soymido* Telinga.

All the four species of the noble genus *Swiëtenia,* are lofty trees, remarkable for the excellent quality of their wood. The three following are indigenous in *Hindustàn.* 1. *S. Febrifuga,* which we have inserted in the catalogue, on account of the medicinal qualities of its bark. 2. *S. Chickrassa,* (ROXB.) which affords the wood of that name, esteemed by the cabinet-makers, in *Calcutta,* as little inferior to mahogany. 3. *S. Chloroxylon,* (ROXB.) the wood of which, from the closeness of its grain, and its beautiful bright yellow colour, has obtained, from the *English* in *India,* the name of *Satin-wood.* The 4th. *S. Mahogani,* (W.) is a native of *Jamaica* and *Spanish America.* The excellence of the wood of this tree, and its superiority to every other, for all domestic purposes, is universally allowed.

The *Swietenia Febrifuga* is indigenous in the mountainous parts of the *Rajahmundry Circar.* It is a large tree, rising with a straight stem to a great height. The wood is remarkably durable; and, on that account, is preferred, by the *Telingas*, to any other, for the timber-works of their temples. The bark is covered with a rough grey cuticle, and internally is of a light red colour. It has a bitter, united with an astringent taste; both in a strong degree, particularly the bitter. We are indebted to Dr. ROXBURGH for the discovery of its medicinal virtues. Judging from its sensible qualities, that it might possess a considerable tonic power, and prove a useful remedy for the intermittent fever, he made trial of it in several cases of that disease, and found it fully to answer his expectation. With the view of further investigation, he afterwards sent a quantity of the bark to *England*, where it was tried in the hospitals, with equal success, and considered as a valuable substitute, in many cases, for the *Cinchona*. On that account it has been received by the *Edinburgh* college into their pharmacopœia, together with its congener, the *Swietenia Mahogani*, with which, in its properties, it nearly coincides. See Dr. DUNCAN's tentam: Inaug. de *Soymida*: *Edinb.* 1794; and the *New Edinb. Disp.* 1806.

The *Swietenia Febrifuga* is not a native of *Bengal*; and therefore is little known, either to the *Hindu* or *European* practitioners here. I have been informed, however, that it was found, by the late Dr. KENNEDY, in the hills to the southward of

Chunar, where it was called, by the natives, *Rohuna*, and it is probable that this valuable tree may be discovered in the mountainous districts of some of the other upper provinces.

TAMARINDUS INDICA. (W.) *Amli*(1) H. *Amlica* S.
MURRAY, II. 552.
WOODVILLE, III. 544.
TERMINALIA BELLERICA. (ROXB. MS.) *Bahérá*(2) H.
[*Vibhítaca* S. *Belílej* Arab. *Belíleh*. Pers.
TERMINALIA CHEBULA. (W.) *Har*(3) and *Hara*(4) H.
[*Harítaca* S. *Ahlílej* Arab. *Halíleh* Pers.
The unripe fruit, *Zengi Har*(5) H.

The fruit of the *Phyllanthus Emblica* has been already noticed, as one of the kinds of the *Myrobalans* of the writers on pharmacy. Another kind, the *Belleric*, is the dried ripe fruit of the first species of *Terminalia* here inserted. It is about the size of an olive, a yellowish grey colour, obovate shape, and marked with five longitudinal furrows. In sensible and medicinal qualities, it coincides with the other kinds. The second species, the *Terminalia Chebula*, yields several different kinds of *Myrobalans*; different names having been given to the drupe, according to its degree of maturity, when taken from the tree. Those chiefly used in medicine, are the *Har* and the *Zengi Har*. The *Har* is the dried ripe fruit. It is the largest of the *Myrobalans*, of an oblong, ovate shape,

---

(1) *Imlee.* (2) *Buhera.* (3) *Hur.* (4) *Hura.* (5) *Zungi Hur.*

marked with five furrows and five ridges alternately. It is sometimes used medicinally as a gentle purgative, but more frequently employed for domestic purposes, particularly by the dyers, who consume large quantities of it for preparing the cloth to receive the colours. See As. Res. IV. 41.

The *Zengi Har* is the *Indian,* or black *Myrobalan,* of the pharmaceutical authors. It differs from the other kinds in having scarcely the rudiments of a nut, being the fruit dried in a half ripe state.* It is of an oblong, pointed shape, about

---

* It was not until very lately that I could obtain any information respecting the tree which affords the *Zengi Har;* the *Hindu* druggists, to whom I applied, not having been able to give me any account of it. Dr. ROXBURGH, to whom I mentioned this circumstance, on examining the drug, conjectured it to be the unripe fruit, of some species of *Terminalia.* The justness of this conjecture was soon afterwards confirmed, on our inspecting the unripe drupes of a *Terminalia Chebula* in the botanic garden, the appearance of which corresponded exactly with that of the *Zengi Har;* and which, on being dried, proved to be that very fruit.

The uncertainty in which the writers on the *Materia Medica* still continue, respecting the trees which yield the different kinds of *Myrobalans,* appears from the following remark of Professor MURRAY, (Ap. Med. VI. 235.) "De reliquarum (*Myrobalanorum*) specie botanicâ nihil certi pronuntiari "potest, quin adhuc disputatur utrum ex diversis arboribus petitæ sint, an potius ex eâdem." A considerable degree of light will be thrown on the subject, by the following extract from a *Persian* treatise on medicines, the *Mekhzen-ul-Adviyeh* of MUHAMMED HOSEN SHIRA'ZI, communicated to me by the kindness of Mr. COLEBROOKE; and which, had I received it sooner, would have saved me the trouble of inquiring respecting the *Zengi Har.*

Under the head *Ahlilej* (the *Arabick* name answering to the *Persian Halileh*) the author distinguishes the following kinds, as the produce of the same tree (*Terminalia Chebula*) gathered at different degrees of maturity.

1. *Halileh Zira,* gathered when the fruit is just set. Being dried, it is about the size of the *Zira.* (*Cumin seed.*)

2. *H. Jawi,* when more advanced. It is the size of a barley-corn. (*Jaw.*)

the size of a pistachio nut, of a deep black colour, and a firm, compact substance. Its taste is bitterish, and strongly astringent. The *Zengi Har* is, as far as I can learn, more frequently used in medicine, by the natives, than any of the other *Myrobalans* being very generally employed by them as a purgative. It operates briskly, but without occasioning heat or irritation. Persons liable to redundancy of bile, habitual costiveness, or any other complaint which requires the frequent use of gentle laxatives, will find this one of the most convenient which they can use.

The only remaining *Myrobalan* noticed by the writers on pharmacy, is the *Citrina*. The tree which yields this sort has not yet been described, but there are now growing in the botanic garden some young plants of it (raised from seeds brought from the *Malabar* Coast,) which from their habit, Dr. Roxburgh thinks will prove to belong to the genus *Terminalia*.

Trigonella Fænum Græcum. (W.) *Mét'hi*(1) H. *Mét'hi* S.
Murray, II. 447.
Woodville, III. 487.

---

3. *H. Zengi, Hindí* or *Asued;* when the young fruit is still further advanced. Being dried, it is of the size of a raisin, and is black; whence its name. (*Asued* black, or *Zengi* negro.)

4. *H. Chíní*, gathered when the nut has acquired some degree of hardness. The dried fruit is of a green colour, inclining to yellow.

5. *H. Asfer*, when approaching to maturity. The fruit, when dry, is of a reddish yellow; whence the name. (*Asfer*, yellow.)

6. *H. Cábulí*, when the fruit is come to full maturity.

(1) *Met'hee.*

Valeriana Jatamansi. (Roxb.) *Jatamánsi* H. *Jatamánsi* S.

The vegetable which affords the *Indian Nard,* so celebrated by the ancients, as a perfume, remained altogether unknown to naturalists, until it was discovered by the late Sir William Jones, who, valuable as his time was, considered the subject as not unworthy of his inquiry; and, with his usual accuracy of research, proved, beyond all question, that the *spikenard* of the ancients is the plant, called, by the *Arabians, Sumbul-ul-Hind;* and, by the *Hindus, Jatamánsi.* See As. Res. II. 405, and III. 105, 433. It is a species of valerian, and a native of *Napal* and *Butan.* The perennial, hairy portion of the stem, immediately above the root, is the part which, when dried, is so highly esteemed as a perfume; and which is also used in medicine. The *Hindu* physicians prescribe it, chiefly, in diseases of the bowels; but, as it strongly resembles, in taste, smell and flavour, the officinal valerian, there is reason to expect that it will be found equally efficacious with that root, as an antispasmodic, in epilepsy, hysteria, and other convulsive disorders.

Vitex Negundo. (W.) *Nisinda* and *Samb'hálu*(1) H.
[*Sind'huca* and *Sind'havara* S.

Lagondium Litoreum. Rumph. Amb. IV. 51. tab. 19.
Bemnosi Rheede. Hort. Mal. II. 15. tab. 11.

---

(1) *Sumbhaloo* or *Sumaloo.*

This elegant shrub is very generally cultivated in *Hindustàn,* as well on account of its beauty, as for its valuable medicinal qualities. It delights in a watery situation, and is readily propagated by cuttings.*

The leaves of the *Nisinda* have a better claim to the title of discutient, than any other vegetable remedy with which I am acquainted. Their efficacy in dispelling inflammatory swellings of the joints, from acute rheumatism, and of the testicles, from suppressed gonorrhœa, has often excited my surprize. The success with which the natives employ them, in these complaints, has induced some *European* practitioners to adopt the practice, and I hope it will come into general use. The mode of employing the leaves is simple. A quantity of them, pulled fresh from the tree, is put into an earthen pot, and heated over the fire, to as great a degree as can be borne without pain. They are then applied to the part affected, in as large a quantity as can be conveniently kept on by a proper bandage,

---

* The following curious remark of A COSTA, on the facility with which this tree is cultivated, shews the high estimation in which the *Negundo* was held in his time: "Adeo frequens est hujus arboris usus ad medendum in "illis regionibus, ut nisi Deus præcisos ramos multiplici fætura renasci "faceret, jam diu fuissent consumptæ arbores, aut certé maximi pretii "nunc essent." He ought not, however, to have ascribed its being so much in request solely to its medicinal virtues, having before told us. "Mulieres "horum foliorum decocto omni tempore universum corpus lavant; tanta-"que invasit persuasio apud illas *Negundi* folia, flores et fructus, utilia "esse ad juvandum conceptum, ut eum qui contrarium persuadere conetur "lapidibus obruturæ sint." A COSTA, Aromat. lib. interpret. CLUS, p. 286.

and the application is repeated, three or four times a day, until the tumor is dispelled.

II. MEDICINAL DRUGS.

I. VEGETABLE.

The following vegetable drugs are imported into *Hindustàn* from the neighbouring countries, none of the plants which yield them being either indigenous, or found in a cultivated state in the *Peninsula*. The drugs themselves, however, are in common use with the native practitioners, and sold in all the principal bazars.

Anise Seed. *Sónf* H. *Satapushpá* S.

Pimpinella Anisum. { Murray, I. 428.
Woodville, III. 490.

Asa foetida. *Hing*(1) H. *Hinga* S.

Ferula Asa fœtida. { Murray, IV. 358.
Woodville, I. 22.

Benzoin. *Lubán*(2) H. and Arab.

Styrax Benzoin. { Murray, IV. 540 and 659.
Woodville, II. 200.

Cajeput Oil. *Cajuputu*, Malay.

Melaleuca Leucodendron. { Murray, III. 313.
Woodville, IV. 44.

Melaleuca Cajuputi. Ph. Lond. 1809.

(1) *Heeng.* (2) *Looban.*

CAMPHOR. *Cafur*(1)H. *Carphura* S.

Laurus Camphora. { MURRAY, IV. 415. WOODVILLE, IV. 66.

CHINA ROOT. *Chób Chíní*(2) H.

Smilax China. { MURRAY, I. 490. WOODVILLE, IV. 66.

This root was formerly held in high estimation, in *Europe*, as a remedy for the venereal disease; but has long been superseded, by its congener, the *Smilax Sarsaparilla*; yet this last has been, by some authors of great authority, considered as a very inert substance, and scarcely possessing any medicinal virtue whatsoever.* Those who judge more favourably of its efficacy, may, in cases where it cannot be procured, have recourse to the *China root*, as a substitute. Dr. WOODVILLE, after observing that, "like the *Sarsaparilla*, the "*China root* contains a considerable share of bland "nutritive matter," adds, "that it appeared to "him not less adapted to the auxiliary purposes "of medicine."† If the sanative virtue of these roots depends on this nutritive matter, which is probably the case, the *China root* would seem to claim the preference; as it contains it in a much larger proportion, amounting to upwards of half the weight of the root;‡ but there is much difficulty in estimating the comparative efficacy of

(1) *Kafoor.* (2) *Chob Cheenee.*

* J. HUNTER. Ven. Dis. p. 371. CULLEN. *Mat. Med.* p. 200. DUNCAN, *Edinb.* New Disp. Ed. 1806.

† Med. Bot. IV. 67. ‡ AIKIN's LEWIS. *Mat. Med.* II. p. 321.

medicines of such moderate activity as the two in question. The *China root* was formerly much used in the hospitals here; and, as far as I could judge from my own experience, its utility, either as an auxiliary to mercury, or for improving the general health, after the use of that remedy, is at least equal to that of the *Sarsaparilla*.

CLOVES. *Laung*(1) H. *Lavanga* S.

Caryophyllus Aromaticus. { MURRAY, III. 333. / WOODVILLE, II. 366.

COLUMBO ROOT. *Kalumb*, Mosambique.

Radix Colombæ. { MURRAY, VI. 153. / WOODVILLE, IV. 164. / Asiat. Res. X. 385.

See the interesting account of this valuable root in the 10th volume of the Asiat. Res. It is to be hoped, that by Dr. BERRY's meritorious exertions, we may soon have the plant cultivated in this country.

CUBEBS. *Cubab Chini*(2) H.

Piper Cubeba. MURRAY, V. 37.

GALLS. (Alleppo) *Maju P'hal*(3) H. *Máju P'hal* S.

Quercus Cerris. MURRAY, I. 102.

Quercus Robur. WOODVILLE, II. 346.

GAMBIR. *Gambir* H. from the Malay.

Uncaria Gambeer. ROXB. *Pl. Cor.* III.

Funis Uncatus. RUMPH. *Amb.* V. 63.

Nauclea Gambir. HUNTER, Lin. Trans. IX. 318.

This substance is used, by the inhabitants of the *Malay* countries, for manducating with the *Betel* leaf and *Areca* nut, in the same manner as the

(1) *Luang.* (2) *Koobab Cheenee.* (3) *Majoo P'hul.*

Catechu is, by the natives of *Hindustàn*. It is prepared from the leaves of the shrub above referred to, (which belongs to a genus nearly allied to the *Nauclea)* in two different modes. 1. By boiling the leaves, and inspissating the decoction. 2. By infusing the leaves, in warm water, for some hours, when a fæcula subsides, which is inspissated by the heat of the sun, and formed into small cakes. The *Gambir,* prepared in this last mode, is by far the best. In appearance, and sensible qualities, it resembles the *Catechu,* as also in its medicinal properties. Its taste is powerfully astringent, and at first bitter, but afterwards sweetish. Tried by the gelatine test, the *Gambir* appears to contain more of the *Tannin* principle, than any other vegetable astringent; and, were it not for its high price, would be a most valuable material for the preparation of leather.

Gamboge. *Gahkatu,* Singalese.
Stalagmitis Gambogioides. Murray, IV. 106 & 654.
Manna. *Shirkhissht*(1) H. and P. *Terenjabín,* Arab.
Manna Persicum. Fothergill, Phil. Tr. XLIII.47.

The manna sold in the bazars here, is imported from *Bussorah,* and is the same with that described by Dr. Fothergill, in the paper to which I have referred. The plant which yields it, is supposed to be the *Hedysarum Alhagi* (L.) It is a very

(1) *Sheerk'hisht.*

impure kind, and far inferior, in quality, to the *Calabrian* manna.

Myrrh. *Murr* and *Ból*, H. *Bóla* S.

Myrrha. { Murray, VI. 213. / Woodville, IV. 167.

Nutmegs. *Jáéphal*(1) H. *Játiphala* S.

The Mace. *Jawatri*(2) H. *Játipatrí* S.

Myristica Aromatica. Murray, VI. 135.

Myristica Moschata. Woodville, II. 363.

Rhubarb. *Révand Chíní*(3) H.

Rheum Palmatum. { Murray, IV. 362. / Woodville, I. 127.

Sago. *Sábudáná* H.

Sagus, Rumphii. Murray, V. 13.

Sago is procured from the trunks of several other palms, beside that mentioned by Murray. An excellent kind is prepared from the tree called, by Rumphius, *Gomutus Gomuto, (Amb.* I. 57.) and by Dr. Roxburgh, *Saguerus Rumphii*, (MS) This tree is also valuable, on account of the black fibres which surround the trunk at the insertion of the leaves; which afford a stronger and more durable cordage for ships, than any other vegetable substance.

Salep. Salib *Misri*(4) H. and Arab.

Orchis Mascula. { Murray, V. 278. / Woodville, II. 246.

Scammony. *Sukmúnya*(5) H. and Arab.

Convolvulus Scammonia. { Murray, VI. 746. / Woodville, I. 13.

---

(1) *Ja,ephul.* (2) *Juwutree.* (3) *Rewund Cheenee.*
(4) *Salib Misree.* (5) *Sooqmoouniya.*

Senna Leaves. *Sená Mecci*(1) H. *Sená* Arab.

Cassia Senna. { Murray, II. 505. Woodville, III. 446. }

2. MINERAL.

A. Metallic.

Lead. *Sisa*(2) H. *Sisaca* S.

The white oxide, *Saféda* H.

The red oxide, *Sindúr*(3) H. *Sindúra* S.

The semivitreous oxide, *Murdár Seng*(4) H. & P.

Iron. *Lóha* H. *Lóha* & *Ayas* S.

The Carbonate, *Kit'h*(5) H. *Mandura* & *Sinhana* S.

The Sulphate *Casis*(6) H.

Copper. *Támbá* H. *Támra* S.

The Subacetite, *Zangár* & *Pitrai* H. *Pítalatá* S.

The Sulphate, *Tutiya*(7) H. *Tutt'ha* S.

Tin. *Rángá* H. *Ranga* & *Trapu* S.

Antimony.

The Sulphuret, *Surmeh*(8) H. *Saubira* S.

The proper grey ore of antimony is imported from *Napal,* but a galena or sulphuret of lead, is frequently sold for it in the bazars, under the name of *Surmeh.*

Arsenic.

The white oxide, *Samul-k'har*(9) H. *Sanc'hya* S.

The yellow Sulphuret, *Hartál*(10) H. *Haritála* S.

The red Sulphuret, *Mansil*(11) H. *Manah Sila* S.

Quick-silver. *Páru* H. *Párada* S.

The red Sulphuret, *Shengerf*(12) H.

A sub-muriate, *Rascapúr*(13) H.

---

(1) *Suna Mukkee.* (2) *Seesa.* (3) *Sindoor.* (4) *Moordar-Sung.* (5) *Keet'h.* (6) *Kusees.* (7) *Tootiya.* (8) *Soormu.* (9) *Sum-ool-Khar.* (10) *Hurtal.* (11) *Munsil.* (12) *Shungurf.* (13) *Ruskupoor.*

Shengerf, or factitious cinnabar, is prepared by the natives in a very simple mode. The quicksilver and sulphur are first triturated together, until a black sulphuret is formed, which is put into a glazed earthen pot, similar to those commonly used for dressing victuals. Over this, another vessel, of the same kind, is placed, inverted, and luted to it with clay. Fire is then applied to the undermost vessel, and continued until the whole of the contents is sublimed. The apparatus is then suffered to cool; when a cake of cinnabar is found adhering to the inner surface of the uppermost pot.

Shengerf is used, internally, by the native practitioners, as an antispasmodic, and for the cure of cutaneous diseases; but it is employed much more efficaciously by them in fumigation, for such cases of the venereal disease as are attended with ulcers in the nose, mouth and throat. The fumigation is conducted in the usual mode, by making the patient, with a blanket thrown over him, inhale the fumes of the *Shengerf* thrown on red hot iron. In this mode, the cure is performed very rapidly, but it frequently causes a violent and dangerous ptyalism; nor is the patient always secured by it against a relapse of the disease.

Rascapúr is another mercurial preparation, in great estimation, and much used by both the *Hindu* and *Muhammedan* practitioners. There are various modes of preparing it, but none of them essentially different from the others. In all of them quick-silver and *Muriate* of *Soda* are employed in equal parts, with the addition of either *Sulphate* of *Alumine* or *Sulphate* of copper. By the kindness of Dr. HUNTER I have now lying before me three different processes for making *Rascapúr*; one taken from a *Persian*, and the two others from *Sanscrit* pharmacopœias. The first, which is the simplest and least uncertain of the three, is literally as follows:

"Take quick-silver, Armenian Bole; Alum, "('some prefer blue vitriol, but alum is better') "Rock Salt, of each nine parts. Rub the whole "in a mortar with water, and let them harden. "Then put the mass into a glazed earthen vessel; "and place inverted, above it, another similar vessel, plastered with ashes, and the milk of *D'hatúra*. Lute them together with Philosopher's clay, "and keep them three days and three nights in a "fire made with cow dung. Then let the vessels "cool, and take out what adheres to the bottom "and sides of the upper vessel. This is the *Rascapúr*."

The quick-silver, in this preparation, is combined with a less proportion of the muriatic acid, than in corrosive sublimate, but with a much greater proportion of it than in calomel. It is used, by the native practitioners, for all the purposes for which the two preparations, just mentioned, are employed by the *European*. It requires, however, to be prescribed with great caution, as it is not only one of the most powerful mercurials that can be ventured on for internal use, but uncertain in its strength, on account of the different processes by which it is made. *European* practitioners need never, I think, have recourse to it ; as quick-silver may always be procured from the bazars, with which, safer, and equally efficacious remedies may be prepared.

B. Saline.

Nitrate of Potash. *Shóra* H. *Yavashára* H.
Sulpuric Acid. *Gandac-ca Atr*(1) H.
Sulphate of Soda. *C'hárá Nún*(2) H.
Sulphate of Alumine. *P'hitcarí*(3) H. *Sp'haticá* S.
Impure Carbonate of Soda. *Sejji-mitti*(4) H. *Sarjicá* S.
Muriate of Ammonia. *Nósáder*(5) H.
Muriate of Soda. *Nemec*(6) H.
Muriate of Soda, fused with the fruit of *Phyllanthus Emblica.* *Bit-laban*(7) *Sochel*(8) *and Cála Nemec*(9) H. *Vída and Sauverchalá* S.

The following process for making this salt, was communicated, by a native druggist, to Mr. Turnbull, at *Mirzapore*, and actually performed in his presence. Mr. Colebrooke in-

(1) *Gunduk-ka-utr.* (2) *K'hara Noon.* (3) *P'hitkuree.*
(4) *Sujee-muttee.* (5) *Nosadur.* (6) *Numuk.*
(7) *Bit-lubun.* (8) *Sochul.* (9) *Kala-numuk.*

forms me that it nearly corresponds with the process which he found described in a *Persian* treatise on medicines. "Fifty six pounds of *Sa-*
"*mur* salt (a *muriate* of *Soda,* got from a salt
"lake of that name) are mixed with twenty
"ounces of dried *Aonlas, (Emblic Myrobalans.)*
"One fourth of these materials is put into a
"round earthen pot, with a narrow mouth,
"which is put on a fire-place made of clay. The
"fire-place has a hole at the bottom, for introduc-
"ing the fire-wood. After the fire has been light-
"ed about an hour, and the materials in the pot
"appear to be melted, the rest of the materials is
"added by degrees. The whole is then exposed
"to a strong red heat, for about six hours. The
"fire is then allowed to die away, and the pot to
"cool; which, upon being broken, is found to
"contain about forty-eight pounds of *Cála Nemec,*
"or *Bit-laban.*"

The *Bit-laban,* or *Bit-noben,* as it is sometimes called, is a medicine in great estimation, with both the *Hindu* and *Muhammedan* physicians; but particularly with the former. It is very generally used as a tonic in dyspepsia and gout, as a deobstruent in obstructions of the spleen and mesenteric glands, diseases to which children, in *Hindustàn,* are peculiarly liable; and as a stimulant in chronic rheumatism and palsy. It is also one of the many remedies employed as a vermifuge. For a further account of this salt, see "A dissertation on the "*Bit-noben*, by JOHN HENDERSON, of the *Ben-*"*gal* medical establishment. 8vo. *Lond.* 1803."

Mr. HENDERSON having carried some of the *Bit-noben* to *England*, it was analysed by Mr. ACCUM, and the result was as follows:

Four hundred and eighty grains of the salt yielded

Black oxide of Iron	6 Grains.
Sulphur	14
Muriate of Lime	12
Muriate of Soda	444
	476
Loss	4
	480

NICHOLSON'S *Journal for August*, 1803.

From this analysis we may conclude, that the virtues of *Bit-laban*, beyond what may be fairly ascribed to the *Muriate of Soda*, depend on the proportion of iron contained in it. A part of this metal was probably obtained, during the process, from the *Myrobalans*.

IMPURE BORATE OF SODA. *Sôhágá* H. *Tancána* S.

C. Inflammable.

SULPHUR. *Gandhac*(1) H. *Gandhaca* S.
PETROLEUM. *Mittitel*(2) H. *Neft* Arab.

(1) *Gund-huk*, (2) *Millee tel.*

This mineral oil is imported from *Persia* and also from the *Burma* country. See an account of the *Petroleum* wells near *Rainanghong*, by Capt. Cox, in the 6th Vol. of the As. Res.

The oil is met with, in the bazar, of very different degrees of purity ; sometimes perfectly limpid and thin ; at other times of a dark brown colour, and of the consistence of syrup. The first sort only should be used in medicine. It has a strong, penetrating, not disagreeable smell, and a pungent, acrid taste. It is very generally employed by the native practitioners externally, as a stimulant in paralytic complaints, and in chronic rheumatism. In this last disease, I can, from my own experience, recommend it as an efficacious remedy ; having found much greater benefit from it, than from the more costly *Cajeput* oil, which I had previously used.

*Amber.** *Cah-ruba*(1) H. and P.

---

* A concrete, resinous substance, is imported from *Bussora*, which passes, at the *Calcutta* Custom-house, and is also sold in the bazar, under the name of *Cahruba* or *Amber;* but which I found, on examination, to be real *Copal,* the resin so much used, in *England*, as a varnish. This substance is used for the same purpose by the coach-makers in *Calcutta.* It resembles so perfectly the finest amber, in colour and texture, that the jewellers make necklaces of it, which pass for those of genuine *Amber*, and from which it is extremely difficult to distinguish them. The *Copal* is, I believe, the produce of the *Vateria Indica*, a tree which grows on the *Malabar Coast.* I was favoured by Dr. Roxburgh with a specimen of the resin of that tree; and found it, both in appearance and chemical qualities, to coincide entirely with genuine *Copal.*

(1) *Kuhrooba.*

3. ANIMAL.

Musk. *Meshk*(1) H. and P.

Ambergrise. *Amber*(2) H. *Ambara* S.

Considerable quantities of this substance are sometimes brought to *Calcutta*, by the commanders of trading vessels; who find it floating on the *Indian Ocean*, or adhering to rocks, chiefly among the *Moluccas* and other islands to the eastward. It is esteemed, by the natives, as the most agreeable of all perfumes, more especially by the *Mahummedans*. Their physicians consider it also as an *Aphrodisiac*, a class of medicines of great importance in their pharmacopœias, but which probably contains not a single article that has any claim to that title.

Honey. *Medhú*(3) H. *Shehed*(4) P. *Medhú* S.

Wax. *Mom* H. and P. *Medhúch-hishta* S.

Lac. *Lác'h* and *Láh* H. *Lacsha* S.

Hirudo Medicinalis. (L.) *Jónc*(5) H. *Jelaucá* S.

Leeches are found, in stagnant waters, in every part of *Hindustán*. In a country in which general bleeding is so much seldomer required or admissible than in cold climates, and where consequently the practitioner must more frequently have recourse to topical bleeding, it is fortunate that this animal, so convenient for the latter purpose, can at all times be procured.

---

(1) *Mushk.* (2) *Umbur.* (3) *Mud* or *Mudhoo* (4) *Shuhud.* (5) *Jonk.*

Melöe Cichorei (L.) *Telini*(1) H.

Mylabris Cichorei. Fabric. Sp. Insect. I. 330.

See in the 5th vol. of the As. Res. a very full and accurate description of this species of *Melöe* by Col. Hardwicke, to whom we are indebted for discovering that the insect is a native of these provinces, and for bringing it to our notice as an excellent substitute for the *Spanish* blistering fly. It abounds in various districts of *Bengal, Bahar,* and *Owde,* particularly in the rainy season; during which it is found feeding on the flowers of the cucurbitaceous plants, and most frequently on those of the species of cucumber called by the natives *Turói*(2) (*cucumis acutangulus* W.) It is also met with on the flowers of the numerous species of *Sida* and *Hibiscus.* The three transverse undulated black bands on its yellow elytra or wing-cases, constitute a conspicuous specific character, by which it is readily distinguished from the other species of *Melöe*; but it should be observed that the breadth of the stripes varies considerably in different individuals, and therefore some entomologists make the Sp. Charact. *Elytra nigra, fasciis tribus flavis,* instead of *Elytra flava, fasciis tribus nigris.**

(1) *Telinee.* (2) *Tooru,ee.*

* The *Melöe Cichorei* is very widely dispersed, being found in all the warm countries of *Europe* and *Asia*, from *Calabria* to *China*, (*Amœnit. Acad.* VI. 138) also in *Egypt* (Hasselquist. *it.* 410 No. 101) and about the *Cape*

Melöe Trianthemæ.

Autennæ. Moniliform, tapering upwards, black.

Head. Gibbous, broader than the thorax, inflected, black, minutely punctured.

Thorax. Ovate, rounded, shining black.

Elytra. ¼ shorter than the body, flexile, black with a steel blue gloss, minutely punctured.

Wings. Length of the elytra, brown, transparent.

Abdomen. Sides of a vivid orange red, with a line of small black dots, one on each segment; the dorsal line and rest of the body nearly of a *Prussian* blue.

Legs. Black, the tibia terminated with two slender spines, the tarsi of the hinder legs 3-jointed, the rest 4-jointed.

The female is nearly twice the size of the male.

This fly, which for medical purposes is fully as valuable as the preceding, I believe to be a new species of *Melöe*; I do not at least find any of those described in the system to which it can be referred. We are indebted for the knowledge of it to Dr. ADAM BURT, who discovered it in the fields around *Muttra,* when he was superintending surgeon of that station in 1809. It abounds in every part of the *Doab,* and in the districts on the right bank of the *Jumna,* which is fortunate, as the other species (the *Melöe Cichorei*) is less frequently met with in that quarter of the country.

---

of Good Hope. (WULFEN. *Insect. Capens. p* 17. *f* 3, 4 & 6.) Naturalists have agreed to refer the *Cantharis* of the ancients to this species, and the following character of that insect by PLINY, which he has evidently transcribed from DIOSCORIDES, makes the supposition extremely probable. Potentissimæ inter omnes (Cantharides) variæ, luteis lineis quas in pennis transversas habent, multum pingues. (NATURAL HIST. IV. 697. *Edit. Harduini* 1685.) vide *Amæn, Acad.* l. c.

The insect appears early in the rainy season. It is seldom seen on the wing, but generally running on the ground, particularly in fields overrun with the common plant the *Trianthema Decandra* (W.) called by the natives *Bis Copra*,(1) which probably furnishes it with nourishment, though it is sometimes observed feeding on the flowers of the *Solanum Melongena* W. (*Baigan*(2) H. *Vártáci* S.) The orange red colour of the abdomen, with the black dot on each of the segments, form a good discriminative specific character.

Dr. BURT having discovered the property which this insect possesses of being a safe and efficacious epispastic, recommended it as a substitute for the *Spanish* blistering fly, and by his meritorious exertions the use of it has been introduced in all the hospitals of the upper provinces.

Although the *M. Cichorei* is more widely spread than the *M. Trianthemæ*, it is not so abundant in any one province as the latter is in the *Doab*, nor have we yet been able to collect the flies of the former species in any considerable number for use; whereas, during last August and September a supply of the *M. Trianthemæ* was gathered sufficient to serve the two medical depôts of *Agrah* and *Cawnpore* for a twelve month.

---

(1) *Bess K'hupra.* (2) *Buegun.*

Both these species of *Meloë*, when applied to the skin, produce effects precisely similar to those caused by the *Lytta Vesicatoria* (L.) for which they will be found perfectly adequate substitutes, whether as external stimulants, as rubefacients, or for raising a complete blister, according to the mode in which they are applied, and much superior in efficacy to the *Lytta* in the state in which that fly is frequently sent out from *England*.

The flies should be gathered in the morning or evening, and immediately killed by the steam of boiling vinegar, after which they should be thoroughly dried by the heat of the sun, and put into bottles to preserve them from moisture.

APPENDIX.

THE following are the cases referred to at page 33d in confirmation of the efficacy of the bark of the root of the *Pomegranate* tree as a remedy for the tape-worm.

Case I.

Communicated by Dr. WILLIAM HUNTER.

DEC. 9, 1805.

" JAMES FOXTON has for four years and nine " months been subject to the *Tænia*, and passed " fragments of it from time to time. Previous to " the first appearance of this complaint, he belong- " ed to a ship in dock, on the side of the river op- " posite to *Calcutta*; and used to drink the water " of the neighbouring tanks. To the use of that " water he ascribes his complaint. It was in the " beginning of the rainy season, when the water " was muddy; but he did not perceive that it had " any particular taste. He has also at present an " intermittent fever.

" *January* 4, 1806.—Proper remedies were
" given him for the fever, from which he has now
" been free for a considerable time. This day I
" directed him to take a tea-cupful of the decoc-
" tion of the fresh bark of the root of the *Pome-*
" *granate* tree, made by boiling half a pound of
" the bark in three pints of water to a pint and an
" half. This he took in doses of from a tea-spoon-
" ful to a table-spoonful without its producing any
" effect.

" *January* 5.—Began early in the morning to
" take the decoction in doses of a wine-glassful
" every half hour, and before eleven, A. M. had
" taken about a pint, without experiencing any
" sickness except a little after the first dose. At
" noon passed two *Tæniæ,* one of which was entire,
" the other broken off near the head. Both to-
" gether measured nearly thirty three feet. For
" about an hour before the expulsion of the worms
" he felt a sense of weight with slight pain in the
" lower part of the abdomen. The worms came
" away alive.

" *January* 6.—Took the remainder of the de-
" coction, which produced a stool with some small
" fragments of the worm ; probably the head of
" the *Tænia* which was broken off.

" *January* 8.—Has passed no more worms ; has
" a good appetite, and says he is quite well."

Case II.

This and the two following cases were communicated through Dr. Adam Burt, by Dr. William Pollock, Assistant Surgeon of H. M. 33d Regiment.

" George Rose, aged thirty, has been in *In-*
" *dia* three years and a half.

" *April,* 1810.—Has passed at different times
" small portions of the tape-worm, to the presence
" of which in his bowels he attributes a constant
" gnawing sensation at the stomach, and a purg-
" ing, which he has had for several days.

" * He took two pounds of the decoction of the
" fresh bark of the *Pomegranate* root, which oc-
" casioned considerable sickness at the stomach,
" without vomiting; and in the afternoon he pas-
" sed an entire worm alive, upwards of fifteen feet
" long. It lived for a considerable time after it
" was passed. At one end it was upwards of an
" inch broad, at the other it tapered to about the
" tenth of an inch.

" The *Diarrhœa* soon ceased, he returned to
" his duty, and he thinks now (5th July) that he
" has entirely got rid of the tape-worm, as he has
" felt nothing of it since."

* The decoction used in this and the two following cases was prepared as directed page 33.

Case III.

" THOMAS SECHER, aged twenty-nine, has been
" five years in *India*.

" *June* 21, 1810.—Has passed for years small
" bits of the tape-worm, and from different medi-
" cines, the nature of which he does not know far-
" ther than that they purged him briskly. He says
" he has at different times passed them some yards
" long.

" Took two pounds of the decoction without
" any sickness, and in the afternoon passed an en-
" tire worm of the same shape and appearance as
" that in the former case, only that it was dead,
" all coiled up into knots, and when unravelled
" measured no less than two or three and twenty
" feet in length.

" He was asked yesterday (5th July) and he
" said he had never since been troubled with the
" tape-worm."

Case IV.

" JOHN ELLWELL, aged twenty-eight, has been
" five years in *India*.

" *June* 21, 1810.—Says that for a long time he
" has been in the habit of passing pieces of the
" tape-worm.

" Took the decoction with considerable difficul-

"ty from sickness at the stomach, and in the after-
"noon passed an entire worm, in shape exactly re-
"sembling the other two, and in length measuring
"upwards of twelve feet.

"Was asked yesterday (5th July) and said he
"thought himself cured of the tape-worm."

Case V.

Communicated by the patient himself, who is a ship carpenter in the employ of Messrs. KYDS. *As nothing can be more satisfactory than his own account of it, I transcribe his letter* verbatim.

"SIR,

"Agreeably to your request I send you a des-
"cription of my case, after taking the medicine
"recommended for the cure of the tape-worm.
"The medicine I took was not prepared exactly
"according to the prescription you gave me, for I
"could not procure the proper quantity of the
"tree. What I took was prepared as follows:
"Two ounces of the fresh bark of the root of the
"*Pomegranate* tree were boied in a pint and a
"half of water down to three quarters of a pint.
"In the morning at six o'clock I took a wine-glass-
"ful, and continued to take a wine-glassful every
"half hour until I had taken altogether four wine-
"glassfuls. I was not able to take any more, it
"had made me so very weak, faint, and sick, with

"a small degree of cramp in both my legs, so that "I could hardly stand. I remained in this situa-"tion until eleven o'clock, and then I threw the "most part of the medicine up again, after which "I got some ease and began to feel a little appe-"tite. At two o'clock I parted with a worm of "twenty-one feet in length, and after that I felt "quite well but very weak. Next morning the "weakness had quite left me, and I was as well as "ever I was in my life.

"I prepared the medicine the night before, as I "thought it would be easier taken if cold than "warm. I have had the complaint for these three "years, and have tried many different medicines, "but without effect, until this last which has prov-"ed successful. As you may wish to see the "worm, I herewith send it for your inspection.*

"I am, Sir,

"Your ob't serv't

"J. CALMAN.

"*Kidderpore, April* 13, 1810."

It appears from this case that the decoction may be administered with effect, though prepared with a much less proportion of the bark than is usually directed. This, for patients of delicate constitutions is a desirable circumstance, and is also worth

* The worm in this case proved to be the *Tænia Solium*, and those of the other cases were probably of the same species.

attending to with a view to economy in situations where the *Pomegranate* tree is scarce.

Two more cases of *Tœnia,* in which the remedy in question was used with compleat success, have lately been communicated to me by the patients themselves, one a respectable merchant in *Calcutta,* the other a gentleman in the civil service, but as the circumstances of these cases were nearly the same with those of the preceding, it is unnecessary to detail them. I shall therefore only mention that in both instances the worms were voided entire within a few hours, after the administration of the medicine.

The facts above stated fully evince the remarkable power of the bark of the *Pomegranate root* in removing the tape-worm, and will, I think, warrant the conclusion that it is a more efficacious remedy for that complaint than any other which has yet been discovered, without excepting even the *Fern root,** the celebrated remedy of Madame NUFFER. The *Fern root* itself is a substance of scarcely any activity, and if used alone would probably be found of very little service, but a dose of calomel and scammony, (as originally directed by Madame NUFFER,) or some other strong cathartic, is generally given to the patient two hours

* *Aspidium filix mas.* SMITH'S, *Flor. Brit.*
Polypodium filix mas. { MURRAY, V. 453 / WOODVILLE, I. 136 }

after he has taken the *Fern root*, and most physicians are of opinion that when a cure is effected, the merit ought chiefly, if not wholly, to be attributed to the cathartic.* Even with this powerful assistance, the *Fern root* often disappoints expectation. The bark of the *Pomegranate root* has not hitherto, so far as I have been able to discover, failed in any one case in which it has been given. I would not however rest its superior efficacy on that ground only, our experience of it being as yet comparatively scanty, but when in addition to that, we take into consideration the activity which it shews immediately on being received into the stomach, and the quickness of its operation in dislodging the worm without the assistance of any other medicine, it seems reasonable to expect that this *Indian* remedy will prove more generally successful than the *Swiss*.

For this valuable acquisition to their Materia Medica, *European* practitioners are indebted to ROBERT HOME, Esq. by whom I was favoured with the following account of the circumstances which brought it to his knowledge.

" My servant TAROO had been long plagued " with the tape-worm, for which he had taken

* See SIMMON'S account of the *Tænia*, &c. *Lond.* 1778.
CULLEN. *Mat. Med.* II. 41.
MURRAY & WOODVILLE, *l. c.*

" many medicines prescribed for him by a *Hindu* " doctor without effect, when meeting one day " with an old acquaintance of his, a *Mussulman* " *Fakír*, named Azim Shah, he accidentally men- " tioned his complaint to him. The *Fakír* im- " mediately said I will cure you; no one else here " can. He accordingly gave him a medicine " which had the desired effect. When I was " troubled with the same complaint in 1804, " Taroo informed me how he had been cured, " and said if I would take the medicine he would " endeavour to get the receipt from the *Fakír*, " which he was certain he could do for a little " money. I begged he would try, and he suc- " ceeded by paying two gold-mohurs. I lost no " time in having the medicines, (a powder and a " decoction) prepared according to the receipt. " I first took the powder, and after it a tea-cupful " of the decoction, which was instantly rejected. " I then took it in the quantity of a tea-spoonful " at a time. Even this small dose excited some " nausea which I endeavoured to keep off by " walking about the room. In this manner I got " down a tea-cupful in the space of two hours. " The sensation which I felt in swallowing it was " as if the mucus of the mouth, fauces and gullet " was compleatly absterged. In a few hours " after I had taken the decoction, I was relieved " from the worm which came away entire, and

" was thirty-six feet in length. I have not since " had any return of the complaint."

November 14*th* 1810.

Mr. HOME, gave an account of his remarkable cure to ALEXANDER RUSSELL, Esq. surgeon in *Calcutta*, and imparted to him at the same time the *Fakír's* receipt for the remedy by which it had been effected. Mr. RUSSELL, after some further proofs of the efficacy of the medicine, communicated the receipt, for the purpose of its being made publick, to Dr. FRANCIS BUCHANAN, who accordingly had it inserted in the IX. No. of the *Edinb. Med. and Surg. Journal*, the publication referred to p. 33.

It is proper to remark that the powder which formed a part of AZIM SHAH's original receipt, having been found to contribute little or nothing to the cure, was soon laid aside by the *European* practitioners, and, as the reader will have observed, was omitted in the five cases above detailed. It was composed as follows:

Seeds of the *Convolvulus Nil*, (W.) *Nīl Culmi* H.
Seeds of the *Butea Frondosa*, (W.) *Palás* and
[*D'hác* H. *Palása* S.

of each, the weight of half a rupee (about 3i ss) to be powdered separately and then mixed, for one dose. This powder the patient was directed to swallow, (having first put a little sugar into his mouth,) previously to his beginning to take the decoction.

FINIS.

INDEX.